Target Slope Measuring System
A guide to better green reading

Developed by Nick Riley, Putting Coach

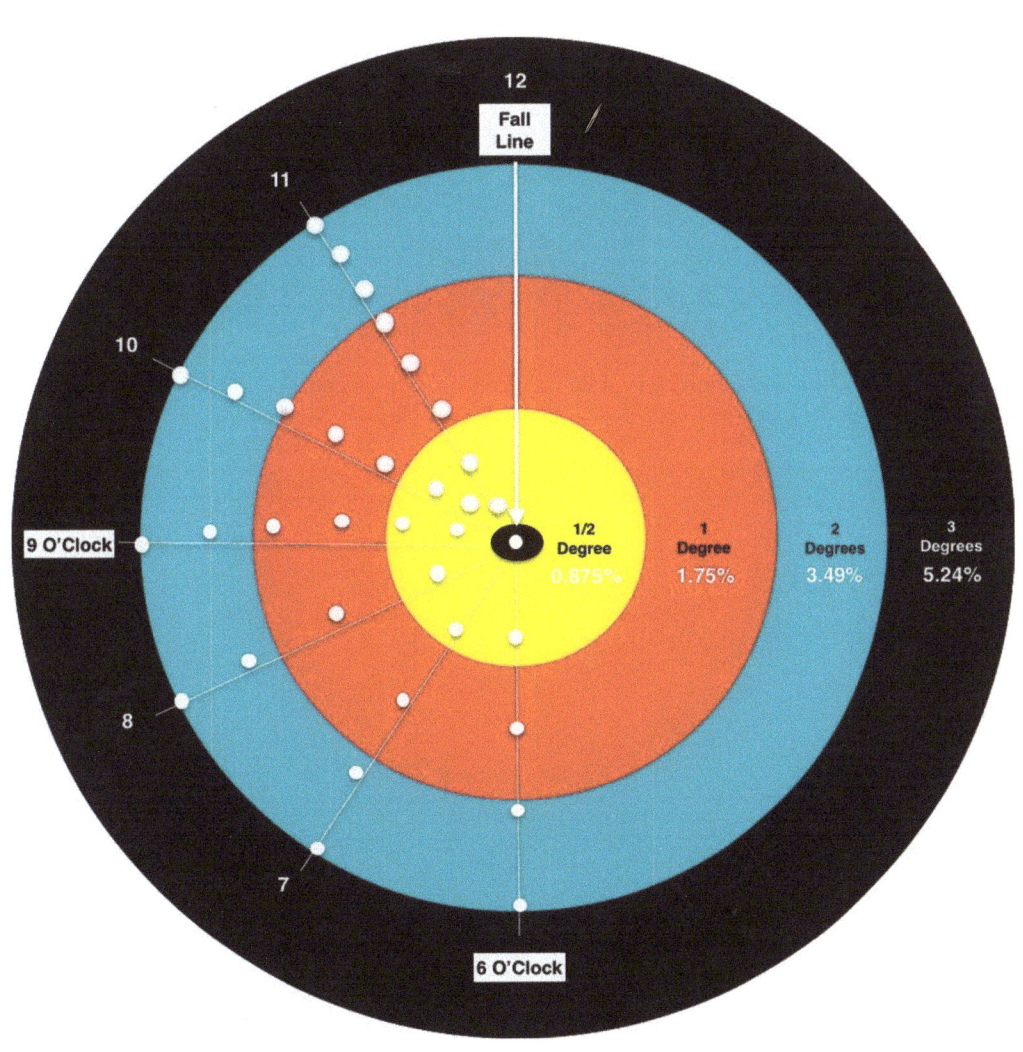

Grosvenor House
Publishing Limited

All rights reserved
Copyright © Nick Riley, 2020

The right of Nick Riley to be identified as the author of this
work has been asserted in accordance with Section 78
of the Copyright, Designs and Patents Act 1988

The book cover is copyright to Nick Riley

This book is published by
Grosvenor House Publishing Ltd
Link House
140 The Broadway, Tolworth, Surrey, KT6 7HT.
www.grosvenorhousepublishing.co.uk

This book is sold subject to the conditions that it shall not, by way of
trade or otherwise, be lent, resold, hired out or otherwise circulated
without the author's or publisher's prior consent in any form of binding or
cover other than that in which it is published and
without a similar condition including this condition being imposed
on the subsequent purchaser.

A CIP record for this book
is available from the British Library

ISBN 978-1-83975-047-2

Introduction

The Nick Riley Putting Academy is a centre of excellence where students receive a unique putting experience. Using scientific tools and hands-on tour experience, we endeavour to help each player find their individual pathway to better putting. Over the past 15 years as a specialist putting coach I have associated and formed alliances with many world-renowned specialists, and I take great delight in sharing some of my findings with you.

Within this book I would like to share some of my theories on green reading and introduce you to my newly developed **Slope Measuring System (SMS).** You will learn to see and assess the extent of the degree of slope on any given putt and, with a little practice on your part, you will soon start to improve your green reading skills and hole more putts.

I am always a little surprised at just how few golfers consider taking a green reading lesson. Did you know that amateur golfers miss as many as 70% of their putts on the low side of the hole? A normal percentage should be 50%, allowing for the process of natural adjustment. Missing more than 50% on a given side is a systematic error. Obviously missing putts on the low side is not the only reason that golfers miss putts; we can simply misjudge the line or even see a slope where there isn't one. Another interesting fact is that 70% of putts missed from inside nine feet are missed due to a misread of the green. I have developed my SMS to address these issues.

For both pros and amateurs, three to seven feet is the distance range that separates good putters from the average. Learning to read greens better WILL make a massive difference to your score.

I believe it is important that a green reading routine suits your own putting process. My SMS has been designed so that it can be used on different levels: you can use it as a stand-alone system, add it as an aspect of layering to a process you may already use or use it on the practice ground to better reinforce your own putting technique.

What is the SMS technique?

The aim of the system is to help you judge the size of a slope and see a slope when it's not easily visible. By identifying the degree of slope, you will learn to intuitively recognise the desired shape of the putt, which will assist you in picking the correct line and thus HOLE MORE PUTTS!

As a putting coach, I work very hard to keep putting as instinctive as possible; this new system has been developed with that same mantra. No system can be perfect, as you don't always have a perfect slope with the exact same degree all the way down your line. Crucially, the speed of the putt will also make a massive difference to the amount of break. Therefore, you will still need to observe the putt and make your own judgment.

Contents

Introduction iii

Overview of the technique 1
Step 1 – SMS Target Explained 4
Step 2 – Check the Putter's Vertical Hang (Plumb Line) 5
Step 3 – Hang the Putter 6
Step 4 – Calibrate the Putter Hang 7
Step 5 – Body Setup and Perpendicular Read Position (PRP) ... 8
Step 6 – Practice and Putting Things Together 10

GOAL SHEET – STAGE ONE 14
Example Goal Sheet 14

Glossary 15
Target 16

OVERVIEW OF THE TECHNIQUE

Before I get stuck into a more in-depth explanation, I would like to give you a brief overview of the SMS by highlighting its key principles.

The SMS works around the idea that the slope of the green changes your body position, allowing gravity and your putter to influence your slope assessment. If you are standing at home on a flat floor with your feet as wide as your shoulders, look down with both eyes open and see that your sternum (the middle of your chest) is directly above the middle of your stance. Your body is in balance – not leaning in any direction as the floor is perfectly flat. I like to call the middle of your stance the '**zero point**'. If you were to hang your putter from your sternum, the putter shaft would point at the zero point (so long as your putter hangs as a plumb line). The hang of your putter will be fully explained later in the document.

When you stand on a side slope, your body mass moves in varying degrees to one side depending on the size of the slope. When you hold your putter from the sternum and hang it like a plumb line, the putter shaft will swing in the direction of the down slope. This might be left or right of the zero point on a side hill putt, as shown in the pictures below.

In Figure 1, I am standing on a balance board which is set on a one-degree slope, this device is an ultra-high-resolution pressure plate which evaluates balance and body mass. In Figure 2 you can see my body mass has moved to the left, 65% of my weight is now on my left foot, this is the effect of standing on a one-degree gradient which in turn moves the upper body to the left as in Figure 1. When positioning the putter in the middle of the chest, the hang of the putter has now moved off-centre, slightly to the left, which indicates that you are standing on a slope.

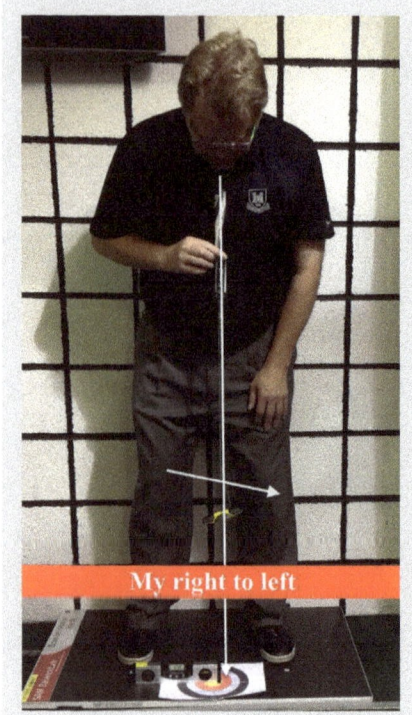

Figure 1

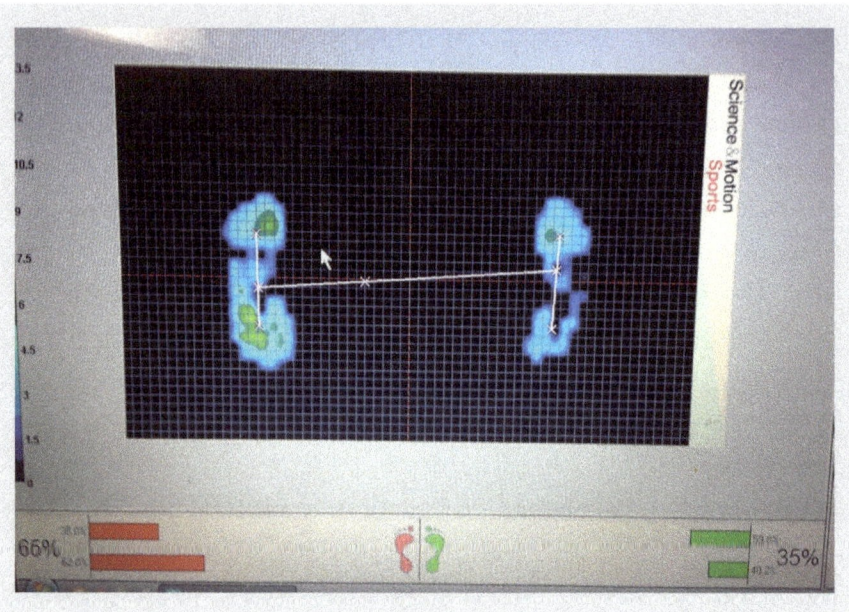

Figure 2

When taking a read on the green, face the hole with your feet as wide as your shoulders and stand at the halfway position of the putt. You will then use my revolutionary 'Perpendicular Read Position' (PRP) technique, which will be explained later in this book. Hang the putter from the sternum, look down, and if the putter shaft swings right or left from the centre of the zero point this will give you a clue to the degree of the slope, and thus the direction in which the ball will roll. If the putter only hangs slightly off centre, then it will be a small amount of break. If the putter hangs near your left or right foot, you will have a bigger break on the ball. The strength of this system is that even the smallest slopes are easily visible when you hang the putter from the sternum.

To cater for these variables in the putter hang, I have devised a simple practice target system that lies between the feet. Once you have hung the putter it will give you a visual cue to help assess the size of the slope.

I'd like to give a quick example of how the system might work with a very small left to right slope on the green. Just imagine you have a four-foot putt; if you are an experienced golfer you may well have a good idea that the ball might move a little from the left to the right, but you're probably not 100 percent sure! If you are inexperienced, or a golfer that goes blind when it comes to green reading, you might not have any idea at all which way the ball will turn. So, stand at the halfway point, facing the hole with your feet as wide as your shoulders. Hang the putter from the sternum in the PRP and if the putter hangs very slightly to the right of the zero point, this means the ball will move to the right. You can now stand over the putt totally confident of your line. You aim the putt just inside the left lip, which will allow for the ball to break slightly to the right and end up in the middle of the hole. Eureka!

This SMS will cover most of your putts, as the average slope on the PGA Tour is 1.1 degrees. There are few slopes of less than 0.5 degrees due to drainage reasons and only 5% of greens have slopes greater than 2 degrees. If you can grasp the difference between a 0.5-, 1- and a 2-degree slope, you will have most of your putts covered.

Hopefully, you now have a basic understanding of the system. Next, remove the target from the back of the book – you will need to test and calibrate parts of the slope measuring system at home before taking it to the golf course.

Follow the in-depth instructions below in order, that you are familiar with all the features of this SMS. It shouldn't take you long to get comfortable.

Let's get started!

STEP 1 – SMS TARGET EXPLAINED

The target included with the SMS programme has been designed to function in two different ways:

1. To calibrate your putter hang position as in step 4.
2. To represent a degree of slope through different colours.

For the explanation regarding the second function above, we are going to assume your zero point is in the middle of your stance.

The coloured rings on the target represent a value we have given to a slope: 0.5 degrees would be a small slope and 3 degrees would be a large slope. The bigger the slope, the more the ball breaks.

The values attached to the different circles:

- If the putter hangs over your zero point (the middle of the yellow bullseye) you would have a straight putt.
- If the putter hangs slightly off the centre of the zero point, but is not in the red circle, it would be a 0.5-degree slope. (0.875%)
- Within the red circle – 1-degree slope (1.75%)
- Within the blue circle – 2-degree slope (3.49%)
- Within the black circle – 3-degree slope (5.24%)
- Outside of the black circle – 4-degree slope or more (6.99%)

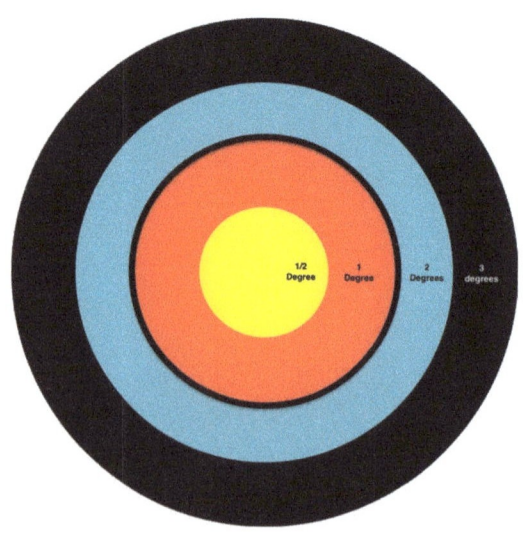

STEP 2 – CHECK THE PUTTER'S VERTICAL HANG (PLUMB LINE)

First and foremost, you need to know in what position your putter hangs vertically. You can check this by finding a straight vertical line such as the side of a wall within a house or a door or window frame – there are normally plenty of options available.

Simply hang the putter in front of you by holding it lightly in the middle of the grip between the thumb and forefinger, letting it hang freely. Look through one eye – this would be the eye which is open when you are firing a gun or looking through a range finder, known as your dominant eye. Rotate the grip between your finger and thumb until the shaft hangs in line with the vertical edge of a wall or a door frame (see figure 1 below). As you rotate the grip, you will see there are big changes in the angle of shaft, so it is *crucial* that this is done correctly, as your putter is the main tool used for this slope reading system.

In Figure 2, the putter is hanging correctly in a vertical hang. Please note the head points to three o'clock with my putter, but other putters could be different. Make a mental note that on every putt you measure, you must hang the putter from the chest; the putter head must always hang in this vertical position.

In Figure 3, the putter head points to seven o'clock. However, because it doesn't hang vertically it will give a false reading.

Figure 1

Figure 2

Figure 3

STEP 3 – HANG THE PUTTER

During the setup it's important that you keep everything consistent.

Hold the putter lightly in the middle of the grip between the thumb and forefinger. With the arm you are using to hold the putter, lightly connect the inside of your forearm to the side of your chest so the putter hangs freely just in front of your sternum. The top of the putter grip should be positioned just below your chin.

Double check that your putter is in its vertical hang position as demonstrated in Step 2.

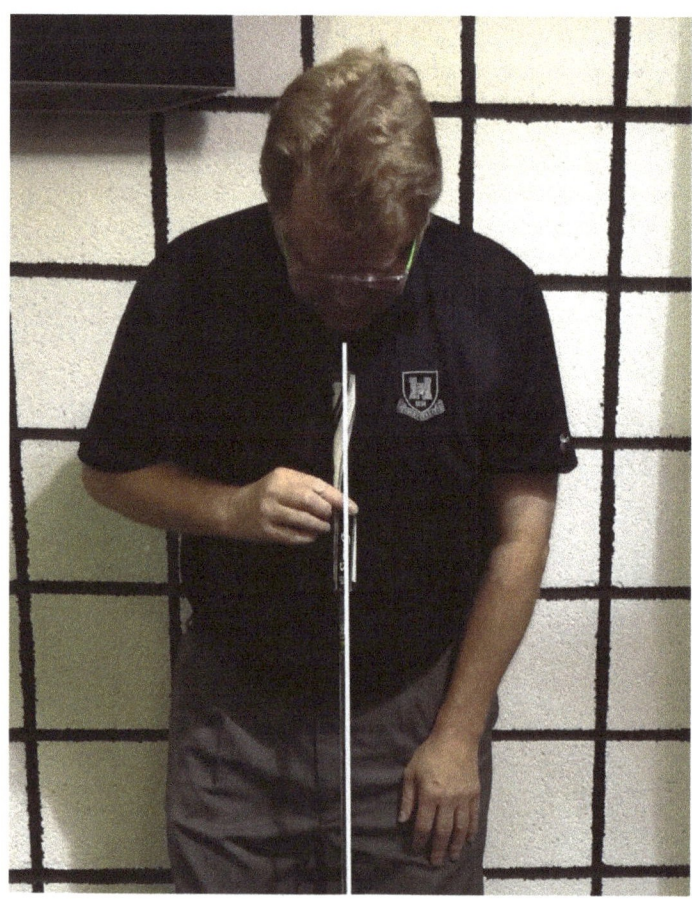

STEP 4 – CALIBRATE THE PUTTER HANG

The idea of calibrating the putter hang is that when you are on the course you know that the zero point is along the toe line and in the middle of the stance. This might be different for some people as they may have a bigger or smaller body type, or have posture issues that affect their balance and the way they stand. On these occasions, the zero point might be off-centre or in front of the toe line; this is okay as long as we know where the zero point is. Make sure the putter can hang freely in all directions without touching your body.

Now we are going to calibrate the putter hang. You need to find a flat surface; normally the best place to do this is indoors. Stand with your feet at shoulder width, place the provided target between your feet and try to position the target so the bullseye is in the middle of your stance and along your toe line.

Take your setup position with the putter hanging from your sternum. You need a slight flex in the knees and a slight bend in the waist, as this will make it easier to look down to see the hang of the putter and a little easier to feel the weight through your feet. The flex in your knees is key to the Perpendicular Read Position (PRP) process and will be explained in Step 5.

See where the putter shaft line hangs; it should point right to the middle of the target along your toe line. You might have to move slightly closer or further away from the target or adjust the way you are bending to get the putter to hang right over the centre position. When viewing the shaft line keep both eyes open.

Everyone's body shape is different and it's fine if it's not possible to get the putter to hang along the toe line – as long as you are aware of your individual zero point.

When you take this to the course, if the putter is hanging left or right of your zero point then you know you are standing on a slope and that the ball will fall in the direction the putter is hanging.

Congratulations! You have just calibrated your putter hang.

STEP 5 – BODY SETUP AND PERPENDICULAR READ POSITION (PRP)

When measuring a slope, stand with your feet facing the target at shoulder width, with a slight flex in the knees and a slight bend in the waist.

When you stand on a side slope your body mass moves in varying degrees to one side depending on the size of the slope. However, your subconscious mind will automatically try to self-correct and your balance system will try to reduce the effect of the slope in order to keep you suitably upright. This happens automatically and will normally rarely be noticed.

On big slopes (Figures 4 and 5) the lower right leg has straightened, locking the knee and the higher leg has flex more at the knee to keep the hips level, which means the body is no longer perpendicular to the slope as in Figure 5, and would reduce how the putter swings in the direction of the downhill slope, making the system inaccurate.

Figure 4: The lower right leg has straightened,

Figure 5: 4-degree slope

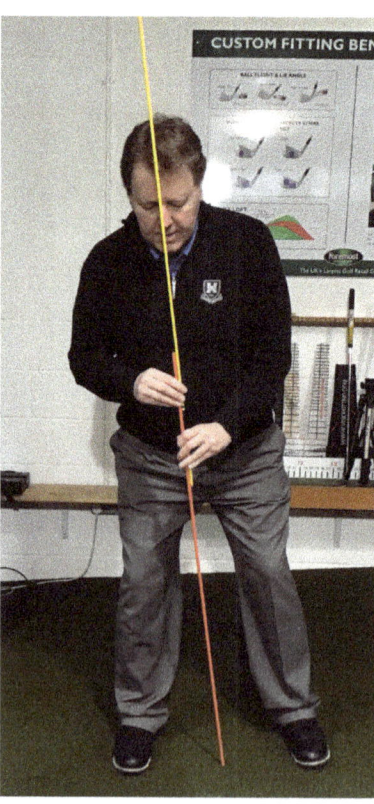

Figure 6: Correct Perpendicular Read

TARGET SLOPE MEASURING SYSTEM

With my new revolutionary perpendicular read position we can correct this unconscious process to keep ourselves vertically upright. **Being perpendicular to the slope is key to this system.**

When getting into the PRP setup, hang the putter as normal but hold the putter shaft with the other hand so it points to the middle of the stance (zero point). Make sure the putter shaft line runs through the middle of your belt buckle, the middle of the chest and through the centre of your head. Make sure both knees are equally flexed, and if you can feel more weight on one side, let your weight settle onto that foot.

You will now be perpendicular to the slope as in Figure 6 and ready to take your measure. Let the putter swing and it will swing in the direction of the downhill to give you the degree of slope. This might seem complicated but after a short while, perhaps after just a few games, you will learn to feel the slope and the flex in your own knees.

Key points to remember when setting up in the PRP

1. Both knees should be equally flexed and level.
2. If you can feel more weight on one side, let your weight settle onto that foot.
3. When taking a measure, hang the putter as normal but hold the putter shaft with the other hand so that it points to the middle of the stance (zero point). Make sure the putter shaft line runs through the middle of your belt buckle, the chest and through the centre of your head.

STEP 6 – PRACTICE AND PUTTING THINGS TOGETHER

I believe it is important that a green reading routine suits your own putting process. My SMS has been designed so that it can be used on different levels: you can use it as a stand-alone system, add it as an aspect of layering to a process you may already use or use it on the practice ground to better reinforce your own putting technique.

I have tried to simplify my advice in this section by only using the tried and tested methods that I have developed over my many years as a professional coach, and those methods that I believe will help your performance on the golf course. Once you have mastered the SMS, I encourage you to work your way through my other green reading insights.

I think it's important at this point to say I would strongly recommend that you practice the system before taking it to the course, as it will take you a while to perfect the SMS setup.

'Remember the laws of physics. For every action there is an equal and opposite reaction. What that means for us is that you have to put the work in to get something back.'

Author Earl Nightingale / Sir Isaac Newton

Practice

Remember that for both professionals and amateurs, three to seven feet is the distance range that separates good putters from the average. Learning to read greens better within this distance WILL make a massive difference to your score.

Accelerate your learning by practicing on different size slopes (0.5-, 1-, and 2-degrees) and practice from different distances (5, 10, 15, and 30 feet), focusing most of your practice under ten feet. By identifying the degree of slope, you will learn to intuitively recognise the desired shape of the putt, which will assist you in picking the correct line and thus HOLE MORE PUTTS!

Important note

In picture 1, we can see the ball tracking into the hole. This is the picture most golfers have in their head regarding a breaking putt.

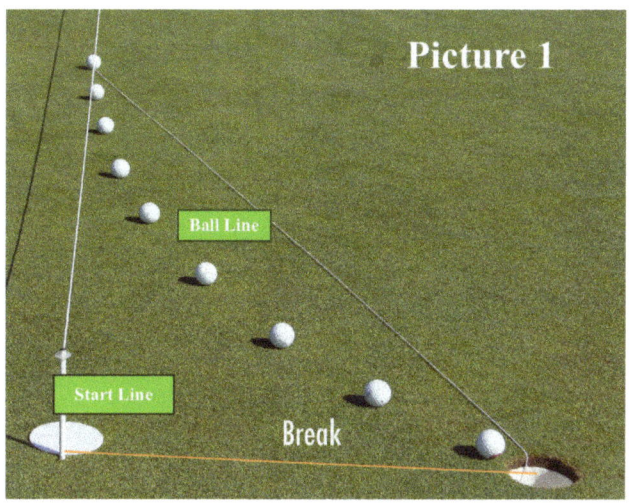

The actual start line as marked by the white string line doesn't match the golfer's perception or picture in their mind, it is much higher than you think, causing them to underestimate the start line value by up to a third! This is one of the major factors that leads amateur golfers to miss 70% of their putts on the lower side of the hole.

As you practice, try to be more aware of this factor and appreciate the start line needed for any given putt.

Goal setting

Your first task is to set your goals and how you plan to achieve them. Focus intensely on your short-term goal with an eye on the long-term goal (please see the example goal sheet).

Key success techniques for better practice:

- What is the smallest single element of this skill you can master and practice until mastered? – Each day try to master one of your short-term goals.
- Choose ten minutes a day rather than a single one-hour session per week.

A short story about achieving your goals.

Think of a ship leaving a harbour. Think of it as you would a whole trip mapped out and planned.

The captain knows exactly where the ship is going and how long it will take – it has a goal and 999 times out of a 1,000 it will arrive at the destination.

Now, let's take another ship just like the first, only with no captain aboard. Let's not give it a goal or destination; we just start the engine and let it go. As you can imagine, it will probably sink before it gets out of the harbour.

The moral of this story is that people with goals succeed because they know where they are going – it's that simple.

Some basic green reading rules

1. Uphill putts break less – Downhill putts break more.
2. Slow greens break less – Fast greens break more.
3. The bigger the degree of slope, the more the ball will break.
4. On any given slope, you will have to allow for more break on your putt as you get further from the hole.

Putting things together

When making your SMS read, I would suggest you stand at the halfway mark of your putt. If you have a ten-foot putt you would stand five feet from the hole, taking care not to stand on your line.

On shorter putts under six feet, it is okay to stand over the ball if you feel uncomfortable straddling the line at the mid-section.

Once you have your degree of slope, view the putt from behind the ball. Work out your target, allowing for any break in the putt; how far do you have to aim left or right?

Are you going to stroke the ball more positively as per the yellow line in the picture, allowing a small amount of break, or are you going to stroke the putt with less pace and lag it as the red line indicates?

Important note – Visualise the path and shape of the putt and the ball going into the hole, then sense the kind of stroke you need to turn the previous images into reality. Having a positive mindset during this process will help.

Once you have your read, move into your setup position, keeping your eyes connected with your intended line.

I highly recommend using visualisation; it is used in many sports and by many of the world's best athletes. Imagery provides a fast track to your subconscious.

Double breaks and two-tier greens

The SMS mid-read point works well when dealing with a putt that has a double break, or if you are putting on a two-tier green. You can take multiple reads to help estimate the slope

Summary

I hope you enjoy using my SMS. Gradually you will learn to see and assess the extent of the degree of slope on any given putt, and with a little practice on your part, you will soon start to improve your green reading skills and hole more putts. Please note that the read isn't always perfect as a slope is not always the exact same degree all the way down the line. You will still need to view the putt and make a judgment.

For further clarification on any part of this book, you can book a one-to-one session with a certified instructor via the following link below.

www.target-green-reading.com

Good luck and thank you for purchasing my Target Slope Measuring System guide.

GOAL SHEET – STAGE ONE

(Example Sheet)

Your first task is to set your goals and how you plan to achieve them.
Focus intensely on your short-term goal with an eye on the long-term goal.

Key success techniques for better practice:

What is the smallest single element of this skill you can master and practice until mastered? – Each day try to master one of your short-term goals.
Choose ten minutes a day rather than a single one-hour session per week.

Date 01/01/20
Short-term Goal

1. Perfect steps 1 to 5 in the SMS.
2. Observe my routine and mindset before and during the putt. What am I thinking before I putt?

Is imagery suitable for me?

Long-term Goal

1. Improve my green reading skills and stop three putting.
2. Lower my putts per round. My average = 33 putts per round. Target = under 30.

Drills and Practice

1. Putt from three to nine feet around the hole in a spiral shape, changing the degree of slope occasionally.
2. Increase the degree of slope for a more difficult routine.

GLOSSARY

Plumb Line – a plumb line, or plumb bob is a weight, usually with a pointed tip on the bottom, suspended from a string and used as a vertical reference line. (With this system your putter is used as a plumb line.)

Sternum – the sternum or breastbone is a long flat bone located in the central part of the chest.

Perpendicular – in elementary geometry, the property of being perpendicular is the relationship between two lines which meet at a right angle (90 degrees).

Borrow and Break – refers to the distance right or left of a straight line to the hole that the golfer must start his putted ball to account for the slope of the green.

Read – the player makes a judgment on how much the ball is going to borrow or break.

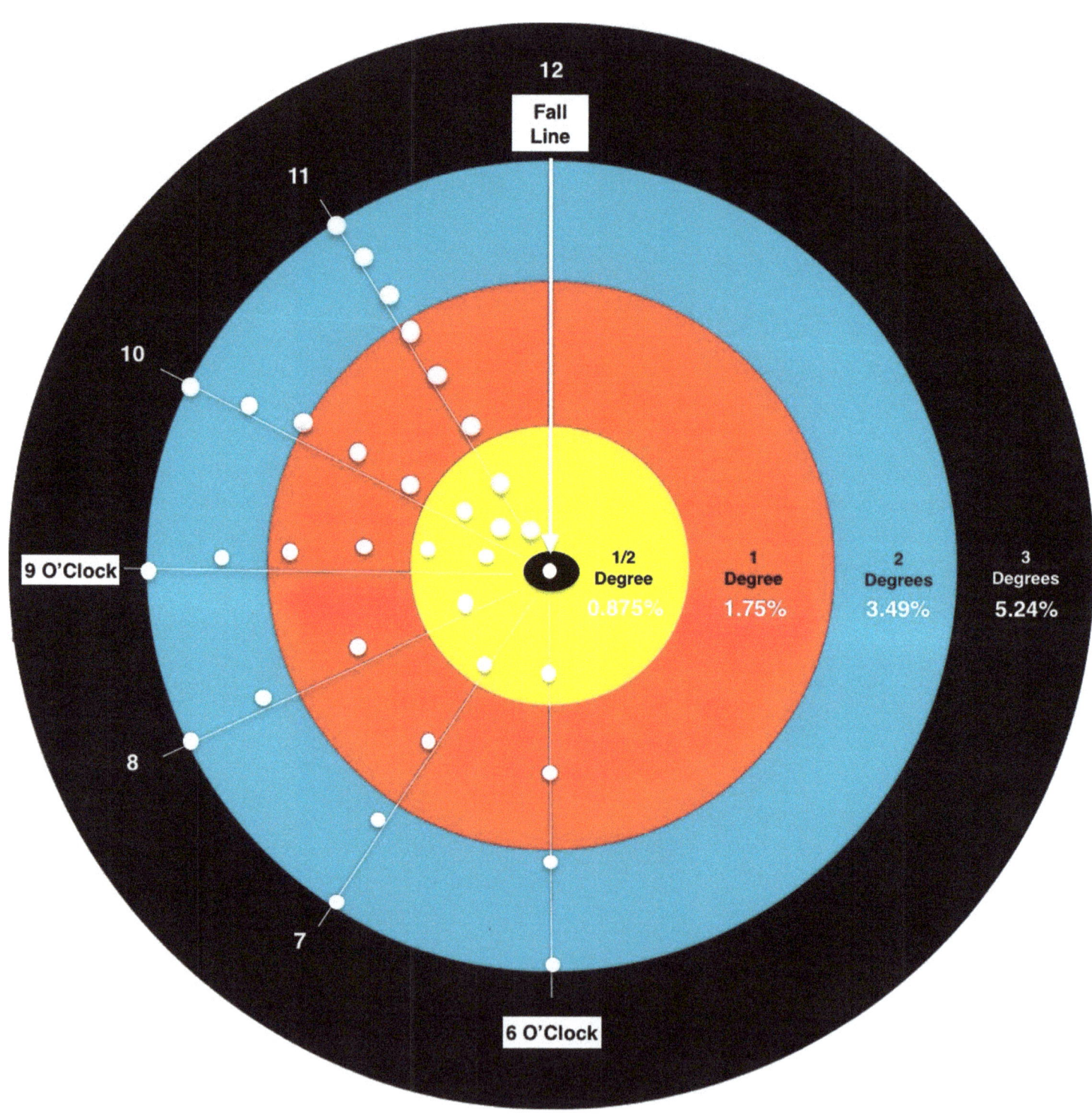

www.ingramcontent.com/pod-product-compliance
Lightning Source LLC
Chambersburg PA
CBHW060925170426
43192CB00024B/2900